© Giulio Russo

Author:
Giulio Russo
www.giuliorusso.com

Introduction	3
Chapter 1 - Negative Words to Avoid	5
Chapter 2 - The Importance of Positive Language	8
Chapter 3 - Tuning into the Customer	10
Chapter 4 - Customizing the Message, Putting the Customer at the Center of Attention	13
Chapter 5 - Empathy and Connectivity, Building Relationships Based on Genuine Understanding	16
Chapter 6 - Persuasive Words, a Guide to the Art of Persuasion in Sales Messages	19
Chapter 7 - Handling Objections, Navigating Resistances with Words of Trust and Competence	22
Chapter 8 - Speaking Clearly and Fluently: The Key to Success in Communication	26
Chapter 9 - The Seller's Body Language	29
Chapter 10 - Punctuality and Reliability: The Foundation of Credibility and Trust	32
Chapter 11 - Customize the Product or Service: The Art of Creating Unique Experiences	35
Chapter 12 - The Importance of Avoiding Inappropriate Jokes in Sales	38
Chapter 13 - Well-Groomed Appearance, Appropriate Attire, and Accessories: Your Personal Presentation	41
End	44

Introduction

Welcome to the best book dedicated to the art of sales, a guide based on the experience of a seller with a decade of experience in the field: Giulio Russo. These pages represent a concentration of knowledge and skills acquired over the years, a journey through the key aspects that characterize the world of sales.

Sales is one of the most dynamic and challenging, yet rewarding, activities one can undertake. It's a world where the ability to communicate, persuade, and understand the customer plays a central role. But it's not just about words or the ability to argue; sales also involve the ability to create authentic relationships, convey trust, and uphold the highest ethical standards.

This book is the result of years of field experience and continual learning. Together, we will explore the fundamental themes of sales, summarized in a simple and understandable way for everyone, such as:

Words to Avoid: We will learn to recognize the words that can compromise a sale and replace them with more effective language.

The Importance of Positive Language: We will discover how positive language can positively influence the customer's attitude and increase the chances of success.

Empathy and Connectivity: We will see how to develop empathy and use words that demonstrate genuine understanding and interest in the customer.

Persuasion in Sales Messages: We will explore the art of using persuasive words to create urgency and increase the appeal of the offer.

Handling Objections: We will learn to manage objections with confidence, using words that convey competence and respect.

Punctuality and Reliability: We will recognize the importance of being punctual and reliable in keeping promises made to customers.

Customizing the Product or Service: We will discover how to tailor what you offer to best meet the needs of your customers.

The Importance of Avoiding Inappropriate Jokes: We will explore ethics and professionalism in interacting with clients, avoiding offensive or inappropriate jokes.

External Appearance and First Impression: We will conclude with the importance of physical appearance, appropriate attire, and accessories in your personal presentation.

In this book, you will find practical examples, tips, and strategies that will help you improve your sales skills and build trustful relationships with customers. My goal is to provide you with a useful and practical tool to excel in the field of sales.

I hope this reading will be of great benefit to you and inspire you to achieve success in this world.
Happy reading and good sales!

Chapter 1 - Negative Words to Avoid

In the delicate world of sales, words can be like arrows hitting the target or boomerangs coming back at you. Avoiding the use of negative words is crucial for maintaining a positive connection with the customer and ensuring the success of the negotiation.

Firstly, eliminate words like "problem" from your vocabulary. This word can generate anxiety and resistance in customers, pushing them to perceive your product or service as a source of inconvenience rather than solutions. Instead, replace "problem" with "challenge", transforming an obstacle into an opportunity for growth.

Another term to avoid is "defect". Using this word can weaken the customer's perception of your product or service. Instead, use expressions like "feature to be improved" to emphasize the possibility of making improvements and demonstrating your openness to continuous refinement.

Also, avoid the word "failure". Its presence can trigger fear in the user, questioning the reliability of your product or service. Opt for "lesson learned" to convey the willingness to learn from past mistakes and improve continuously.

Similarly, be cautious in using words like "unsustainable" or "impossible". These words can suggest limitations and discourage the customer. Instead of declaring something impossible, use terms like "challenging" or "requires effort" to highlight the opportunity to overcome obstacles with dedication and effort.

Avoid terms like "expensive". This word might make the price seem like a burden rather than an investment. Replace it with "investment" to emphasize the long-term value of the product or service you are presenting.

The term "complicated". This word can raise fears in the customer's mind, making them perceive your product or service as overly difficult to understand or use. Replace "complicated" with "simple" to convey the idea that your product is intuitive and easily accessible.

The use of "demanding". This word can make the customer feel overwhelmed or stressed. Instead, use "engaging" to indicate that the experience with your product or service will be engaging and rewarding.

Be cautious in using "limited". In some cases, this word can generate anxiety in the customer, making them think they are missing a unique opportunity. Instead of "limited", use expressions like "exclusive" or "special offer" to create a sense of value without generating undue haste.

Avoid using "mandatory". This word can make the customer feel coerced or under pressure. Opt for "recommended" or "advisable" to suggest an action without exerting excessive pressure.

Conclusion:

Remember that negative language can significantly influence the customer's perception, affecting their purchasing decision. Navigating carefully through the sea of words is essential for creating a positive and lasting sales experience. Be mindful of the words you use and transform the way you communicate to build stronger connections and achieve success in your sales. The next page will focus on more words to avoid and provide strategies for winning language.

Chapter 2 - The Importance of Positive Language

The language we adopt during a sales negotiation is like a brush that paints the image of our offer in the customer's mind. In this context, the use of positive language is fundamental and can make the difference between a successful sale and a customer who walks away. Let's explore the importance of positive language in sales and how it can positively influence the overall customer experience.

First and foremost, positive language creates a welcoming and favorable environment. When a salesperson uses positive words and phrases, it creates an atmosphere that puts the customer at ease. For instance, instead of saying "Don't worry, you won't have problems with our product," the seller might opt for "You will be amazed at how easily our product integrates into your daily life." This slight variation conveys confidence and optimism.

Furthermore, positive language helps to create an emotional bond between the seller and the customer. Empathy is crucial in sales, and positive words can contribute to establishing a deeper connection. For example, a salesperson might say, "I understand how important it is for you to find the right solution," demonstrating empathetic understanding of the customer's needs.

Positive language also has the power to turn objections into opportunities. When a customer raises a concern or doubt, a seller using positive language can address the situation constructively. Instead of responding with a defense, they could say, "I appreciate your attention to detail. I want to assure you that we are here to address any concerns you may have." This response not only addresses the objection but also strengthens the customer's trust in the process.

Another important aspect is that positive language can influence the perception of value. Using words like "advantage," "success," and "solution," the seller can effectively communicate the benefits of the product or service. For example, instead of saying "This product is less expensive than others," the seller might state, "This product offers incredible value for money."

A practical example of the importance of positive language can be observed in the sale of technological products. Instead of highlighting the shortcomings of a device, a seller might focus on its strengths and the positive experiences it can offer the customer. This approach not only encourages the customer to view the product positively but also creates a lasting impact on the brand's perception.

Conclusion:

Positive language is a powerful ally in every seller's toolkit. The careful choice of words can transform an interaction from an ordinary transaction to a memorable experience. The next time you find yourself in the sales room, remember the power of words and how a positive approach can open doors that would otherwise remain closed.

Chapter 3 - Tuning into the Customer

In sales, the ability to tune into the customer emerges as one of the critical factors that separate average sellers from extraordinary ones. This chapter explores the importance of this tuning and provides practical strategies for creating meaningful connections with customers.

The Importance of Tuning into the Customer:

Tuning into the customer goes well beyond mere communication; it's the process of deeply understanding the customer's needs, desires, and even fears. When a seller is truly tuned in, they can tailor their presentation in a targeted way, creating a personalized experience that resonates with the customer.

A customer will feel more inclined to do business with someone who demonstrates genuine interest in them. Tuning into the customer is a sign of respect and attention, key elements for building lasting relationships. It creates fertile ground for mutual trust, which is the foundation of every successful transaction.

How to Tune into the Customer:

1. Active Listening:
A fundamental way to tune into the customer is to practice active listening. Don't just hear the customer's words, but try to understand the underlying meaning. Provide feedback, repeating or paraphrasing what the customer has said, thus demonstrating that you have truly received the message.

Example: If a customer expresses concerns about the battery life of a product, respond empathetically:

"I understand how important it is for you to have a product with reliable battery life. I can assure you that our product has been designed to offer optimal performance in terms of battery life."

2. Ask Open-Ended Questions:

Use open-ended questions to encourage the customer to share more details about their situation and needs. This not only provides valuable information but also shows that you are trying to fully understand their perspective.

Example: Instead of asking "Do you need anything in particular?", try "Can I ask what your main priorities are at the moment? This way I can recommend the most suitable product for your needs."

3. Observe Non-Verbal Signals:

Non-verbal communication is just as important as the words themselves. Observe the customer's body language, gestures, and facial expressions to grasp nuances of meaning that might not emerge verbally.

Example: If a customer seems hesitant while talking about a certain product, you might gently ask: "I noticed you seem to have some doubts. Can I help clarify any concerns?"

4. Adapt Your Language:

Tuning into the customer also requires the ability to adapt your language. Use vocabulary and communication style that resonate best with the customer, avoiding technical terms or overly formal language if it does not reflect their preference.

Example: If you are dealing with a customer who shows a more informal approach, you might say: "I'd love to better understand your needs and find the perfect solution for you.

What can we do together to make this process easier and more satisfying for you?"

Practical Examples of Tuning into the Customer:

1. Scene 1: Electronics Sale

A customer enters an electronics store and mentions they are interested in a new laptop for work. The seller might tune in by asking: "I understand you are looking for a laptop for work purposes. May I ask which specifications you find most crucial for your job?"

2. Scene 2: Clothing Sale

In a clothing store, a customer is looking for a dress for a special occasion. The seller could demonstrate tuning by saying: "It's exciting to find the perfect dress for a special occasion. Can I help you find something that makes you feel incredible for that important day?"

Conclusion:

Tuning into the customer is a dynamic process that requires constant practice. It's an investment that pays off in stronger relationships, more satisfied customers, and ultimately, success in the world of sales. On the next page, we will explore further strategies to refine this skill and create lasting connections.

Chapter 4 - Customizing the Message, Putting the Customer at the Center of Attention

In the complex universe of sales, the ability to customize the message is one of the keys to success. Chapter 4 of our guide focuses on this fundamental aspect, emphasizing the importance of avoiding generic speeches and creating a tailored message for the specific needs of each customer.

The Importance of Customizing the Message:

Imagine walking into a store looking for a pair of shoes. A salesperson approaches and begins talking about the technical features of a wide range of shoes without even asking about your preferred style or size. How likely would you be to make a purchase in that context? Customizing the message is key to avoiding this situation and to creating a meaningful shopping experience.

When a message is customized, the customer feels recognized, listened to, and important. By avoiding generic talk, the seller demonstrates a real commitment to the customer's needs, creating fertile ground for trust and loyalty.

How to Customize the Message:

1. Gather Information:
Customization starts with gathering information. Use previous data, analysis of customer behavior, and information collected during the interaction to better understand the customer's needs and preferences.

Example: An online seller who notices a customer primarily purchasing skincare products could customize the message by offering suggestions on new products in line with their previous purchase choices.

2. Use the Customer's Name:
A simple but effective way to personalize a message is using the customer's name. Referring to the customer by name immediately creates a sense of personal connection.

Example: "Hello [Name], thank you for returning to our store. We noticed you enjoyed our home product offers. Can I help you find something specific today?"

3. Adapt the Language:
Adapt the tone and language of your message to the customer. If you're dealing with a customer who prefers a more formal approach, use appropriate language. If, on the other hand, the customer is more informal, adapt your communication style accordingly.

Example: "We are excited to help you find the perfect product for you" vs "We are here to assist you in finding the product that best suits your needs. How can I help you today?"

4. Link the Product to the Customer's Needs:
Connect the benefits of the product or service to the customer's specific needs. Show how what you are offering directly meets their needs or solves a problem they might have.

Example: "Our range of home products is designed to make your life more convenient and organized. You mentioned you were looking for solutions to optimize space. We have some products that might interest you."

Practical Examples of Message Customization:

1. Scene 1: Online Clothing Sale
An online clothing site, after a customer purchases a winter jacket, might send a personalized email with suggestions on accessories or other items that pair well with the jacket purchased.

2. Scene 2: Beauty Products Sale
A beauty product retailer who notices a customer regularly purchases hair care products could suggest new arrivals or special offers on the customer's preferred brands through personalized messages.

Conclusion:

Customizing the message is a powerful strategy for building meaningful relationships with customers. When a customer perceives that the seller is investing time and energy to understand their specific needs, they are more likely to trust and continue doing business with that seller. On the next page, we will explore further strategies to refine your customization skills and to ensure that every customer truly feels at the center of attention.

Chapter 5 - Empathy and Connectivity, Building Relationships Based on Genuine Understanding

Empathy emerges as one of the most powerful tools for building meaningful connections with customers. In this chapter, we dedicate ourselves to exploring the importance of developing empathy and connectivity during interactions with customers, highlighting the use of words that demonstrate understanding and genuine interest.

The Importance of Empathy and Connectivity:

Empathy means understanding and sharing the feelings of others. When applied to sales, empathy goes beyond merely understanding the customer's needs; it's about recognizing and responding to the customer's emotions authentically. Building connectivity through empathy creates an emotional bond that goes beyond the commercial transaction, contributing to establishing lasting relationships and customer loyalty.

When a customer truly feels understood and supported, their trust in the seller increases significantly. Empathy plays a key role in making this experience authentic. Using words that demonstrate understanding not only creates a comfortable environment for the customer but also shows the customer that the seller cares about their well-being, going beyond just selling a product or service.

How to Develop Empathy and Connectivity:

1. Active Listening:
Active listening is the cornerstone of empathy. When the seller demonstrates that they are listening

attentively, the customer feels valued. Repeat or paraphrase what the customer says to confirm understanding and to show that you are paying attention.

Example: If a customer expresses frustration about a problem, the seller could respond empathetically: "I can imagine how frustrating that must be. I would be too if I were in your situation. How can I help you resolve this issue?"

2. Use Empathy Phrases:
The use of explicit empathy phrases is crucial. Words like "I can understand how you feel" or "I'm sorry you are going through this situation" show the customer that the seller not only understands their emotions but genuinely cares about their well-being.

Example: If a customer talks about a negative experience with a product, the seller could respond with empathy: "I'm sorry to hear you had this experience. I understand how frustrating it can be. I want to find a solution that makes you satisfied."

3. Share Related Experiences:
Where appropriate, sharing personal related experiences can strengthen empathy. However, it is important to do so tactfully and without overshadowing the customer's experience. This creates a sense of connection and shows that the seller is human, not just a sales professional.

Example: If a customer talks about a family challenge, the seller might respond: "I've been through a similar situation myself. I know how challenging it can be. What can I do to help you overcome this challenge?"

4. Express Yourself Authentically:
Authentic empathy cannot be faked. It's essential that

the seller genuinely expresses concern and understanding. Words must be backed by authenticity and true empathy.

Example: If a customer expresses concern about a personal problem, the seller might say: "I'm sorry you're facing this difficult time. I want to assure you that I am here to support you in any way I can."

Practical Examples of Empathy and Connectivity:

1. Scene 1: Technical Support Sale:
A customer calls customer service to resolve a technical issue. The representative could respond with empathy: "I'm sorry you are facing this problem. I understand how frustrating it can be. We will work together to solve it."

2. Scene 2: Luxury Goods Sale:
A customer visits a luxury goods store and mentions feeling overwhelmed by the options. The seller could respond with empathy: "I can understand how the wide range of options might be a bit overwhelming. I want to make this shopping experience as enjoyable as possible for you. Is there something specific you are looking for today?"

Conclusion:

Empathy and connectivity are key to building meaningful relationships in the world of sales. When a customer perceives that the seller is authentically interested in their well-being and understands their emotions, the connection deepens, giving the customer a feeling of trust.

Chapter 6 - Persuasive Words, a Guide to the Art of Persuasion in Sales Messages

In this chapter, we dive into the fascinating world of persuasive words, exploring the use of terms like "exclusive", "limited", and "immediate benefit". These words not only capture the customer's attention but also create a sense of urgency, increasing the appeal of the offer. We will discover the importance of these words in the context of sales and how to personalize the message to make it authentically persuasive.

The Importance of Persuasive Words:

Words have the power to evoke emotions, create desire, and stimulate action. In sales, the use of persuasive words is one of the main elements for pushing the customer beyond mere consideration and inducing them to take action. These words not only communicate the benefits of the product or service but also create a sense of urgency, suggesting to the customer that the opportunity might be limited or exclusive.

The art of persuasion is not just about convincing the customer to buy, but also about doing so in a way that they feel happy and satisfied with their decision. Persuasive words are like little spells that channel the power of the customer's emotions in the desired direction.

How to Use Persuasive Words:

1. Exclusivity:
The word "exclusive" evokes a sense of uniqueness and privilege. Using it creates the idea that the offer is reserved for a select group, making the customer feel special and part of something unique.

Example: "We have prepared an exclusive offer just for our most loyal customers. Do you want to be one of the first to benefit from this opportunity?"

2. Limitedness:

The idea of limitedness creates a sense of urgency and scarcity, prompting the customer to act quickly so as not to miss the opportunity. Words like "limited" or "limited quantity" activate the desire to acquire something precious that might soon be unavailable.

Example: "We are offering a special discount on this product, but the offer is limited. Only for the first 50 buyers. Don't miss this opportunity!"

3. Immediate Benefit:

Emphasizing the immediate benefits of the product or service captures the customer's attention, offering a tangible incentive for the purchase. Words like "immediate benefit" communicate that the customer won't have to wait long to enjoy the advantages of the offer.

Example: "This software will not only improve your productivity, but you will start to notice the benefits from the very first day. Don't miss the opportunity to transform your business today!"

4. Unique Experience:

The word "unique" emphasizes the extraordinariness of the offer, leveraging the customer's desire to experience something special and unrepeatable.

Example: "We have created a unique experience that you won't find anywhere else. Every detail has been taken care of to offer you something extraordinary. We invite you to be part of this exclusive experience."

5. Satisfaction Guarantee:
Security is an essential part of the customer's decision-making process. Words like "satisfaction guarantee" build trust, reassuring the customer that the purchase is risk-free.

Example: "We offer a total satisfaction guarantee. If you are not happy with your purchase within 30 days, we will refund the full amount. Your satisfaction is our absolute priority."

Practical Examples of Persuasive Words:

1. Scene 1: Online Subscription Sale:
"This is an exclusive opportunity for our premium subscribers. You will have access to exclusive content, special offers, and previews of new products. Become a premium member today and experience a completely new shopping experience!"

2. Scene 2: Beauty Product Sale:
"Our beauty product set is available in limited quantity. Only the first 100 customers will have the opportunity to receive an exclusive gift with their purchase. Don't miss this chance to transform your beauty routine with high-quality products."

Conclusion:

Persuasive words are key to stimulating action and creating a sense of urgency in customers. When used with care and authenticity, these words can transform a sales message into an irresistible opportunity. On the next page, we will explore further strategies for refining the art of persuasive words and guiding customers towards satisfying purchase decisions.

Chapter 7 - Handling Objections, Navigating Resistances with Words of Trust and Competence

Handling objections is a crucial art in sales. In Chapter 7 of our guide, we will explore the importance of skillfully managing objections using words that convey trust and competence. We will avoid defensive words and instead focus on reassuring phrases like "I understand your concerns" and "I can assure you that", creating an emotional bond with the customer.

The Importance of Handling Objections:

Objections are inevitable in the sales process. They can stem from legitimate customer concerns, misunderstandings, or emotional resistances. As a seller, your ability to handle these objections can make the difference between a successful transaction and a missed opportunity. Handling objections is not just about solving the problem but also about strengthening the customer's trust in the process and in your competence.

When a customer expresses an objection, it's a sign that they are considering the offer but have concerns. Addressing these objections with empathy and words that convey trust can turn the obstacle into an opportunity to strengthen the relationship and guide the customer towards a positive decision.

How to Handle Objections with Words of Trust and Competence:

1. Understand the Customer's Concerns:
Before responding, it's essential to fully understand the

customer's concerns. Ask questions to obtain more details and show that you are listening attentively.

Example: "I understand you have concerns regarding the cost of the product. Can I ask you to elaborate on which specific aspects are contributing to your concerns?"

2. Avoid Defensive Words:
Avoid words or phrases that sound defensive or minimize the customer's concerns. The goal is to create an open and respectful dialogue.

Example: Avoid - "I don't understand why you think the price is high."
Instead, use - "I can understand how the price can be an important consideration. I want to assure you that we are striving to offer the best possible value."

3. Reassure with Competence:
Show the customer that you have a deep understanding of the product or service and its features. Use words that convey competence and confidence.

Example: "I understand you have concerns about the durability of the product. I can assure you that we have conducted rigorous quality tests and our product is designed to withstand intensive use over time."

4. Offer Solutions and Alternatives:
Propose concrete solutions that can mitigate the customer's concerns. This demonstrates that you are proactive in seeking a resolution.

Example: "If your main concern is battery life, we also have a version of the product with an enhanced battery that can last up to 30% longer than the standard model."

5. Highlight the Benefits:

Reiterate the key benefits of the product or service, showing how they outweigh the customer's concerns. Highlight how the value offered surpasses potential challenges.

Example: "I understand you might be worried about the complexity of using our software. However, many of our customers have found that our intuitive interface and comprehensive support make the software very easy to use, ensuring a quick learning curve."

Practical Examples of Handling Objections with Words of Trust and Competence:

1. Scene 1: Appliance Sale:
Customer: "I'm concerned about the durability of the internal components of this appliance."
Seller: "I understand your concerns about durability. I want to assure you that this model is designed with high-quality components and we have an extended warranty available that can offer you additional peace of mind."

2. Scene 2: Financial Services Sale:
Customer: "I'm afraid of committing to a long-term financial plan."
Seller: "I can understand that making long-term financial decisions can seem like a daunting choice. I want to share with you the details of our plan, highlighting how we can adapt to your evolving needs over time."

Conclusion:

Handling objections requires a delicate balance between empathy, competence, and practical resolution. Using words that convey trust and competence creates an environment where the customer feels understood and supported. On the next page, we will explore further strategies to refine your skills in handling objections and turn resistances into opportunities.

Chapter 8 - Speaking Clearly and Fluently: The Key to Success in Communication

In Chapter 8, we delve into the fundamental aspect of communication: the way we speak. The ability to speak clearly and fluently, using the right tone of voice, is crucial. In this section, we will explore the importance of this aspect and provide methods to improve your communication skills.

The Importance of Speaking Clearly and Fluently:

Communication is the lifeblood of sales. When you are in front of a customer or conducting a presentation, the way you speak significantly affects the customer's perception and your ability to convey information effectively. That's why speaking clearly and fluently is of fundamental importance.

1. Effective Communication: Speaking clearly and fluently ensures that your message is understood without ambiguity. Customers need to have a clear understanding of the benefits of your products or services and the solutions you offer to meet their needs.

2. Credibility and Trust: A confused or unclear way of speaking can erode the customer's trust in your competence. Conversely, clear speech demonstrates professionalism and confidence.

3. Customer Engagement: Fluent communication is engaging. It allows you to capture and maintain the customer's attention throughout the conversation. An engaged customer is more likely to ask questions, listen to your proposals, and, ultimately, make purchasing decisions.

4. Building Connections: The way you speak can affect the emotional connection with the customer. A warm, friendly, and understanding tone of voice can help build a stronger and more lasting relationship.

Methods to Improve Clarity and Fluency of Speech:

1. Constant Practice: As with any skill, practice is key. Find opportunities to practice speaking clearly and fluently. You can do this alone by reading aloud or involving a friend or colleague in your exercises.

2. Pause and Breathe: Speaking too quickly can be hard to follow. Learn to pause and breathe regularly during the conversation. This will help you slow down and communicate more clearly.

3. Avoid Overly Technical Words: If you are selling a product or service that might have technical terms, make sure to explain them clearly to the customer. Avoid excessive use of technical terms without explanation.

4. Use an Appropriate Tone of Voice: Adapt your tone of voice to the context and the customer. For example, when trying to build rapport, use a warm and friendly tone. When providing technical information, use a more professional and confident tone.

5. Avoid Fillers and Interruptions: Overuse of words like "um", "uh", or long pauses can disrupt the flow of communication. Try to minimize these fillers and work on the fluency of your speech.

6. Listen to Yourself: Record yourself speaking and listen to the recordings. This will help you identify areas for improvement, such as pronunciation or clarity.

7. Be Aware of Your Audience: Adapt your speech to your audience. Consider the customer's level of knowledge and interest and modify your language accordingly.

8. Practice Non-Verbal Communication: In addition to words, non-verbal communication is crucial. Maintain open and confident body language, maintain eye contact, and use appropriate gestures to emphasize key points.

Practical Examples:

1. Presenting a Technical Product: If you are presenting a technical product to a customer, try to explain key concepts clearly and using concrete examples. For instance, instead of saying, "This device has a dual-core CPU," you can say, "This device has a powerful processor that allows you to run multiple applications smoothly, without interruptions, and quickly."

2. Creating Connection with a New Customer: When introducing yourself to a new customer, try to use a friendly and welcoming tone. You can say, "I'm excited to help you find the best solution for your needs. I understand how important it is to make informed decisions."

Conclusion:

Speaking clearly and fluently, using the appropriate tone of voice, is an essential skill for success in sales. It not only improves your ability to effectively communicate with customers but also helps build trust, engagement, and emotional connections. By using the methods and practical examples provided in this chapter, you can enhance your communication skills and become a more effective salesperson. Remember that constant practice is the key to success, so continue to practice and refine your way of speaking.

Chapter 9 - The Seller's Body Language

Non-Verbal Communication That Makes a Difference

Non-verbal communication, particularly the body language of the seller, plays a major role in establishing relationships with customers, influencing perceptions, and guiding the success of negotiations. In Chapter 9 of this guide, we will explore the importance of the seller's body language, providing methods to improve your posture and non-verbal communication.

The Importance of the Seller's Body Language:

Body language is a form of communication that often conveys more information than we realize. Its importance in sales lies in the fact that it can either reinforce or undermine the verbal message you are trying to convey. That's why understanding and controlling your body language is crucial:

1. Building Trust: Confident and open body language helps build trust with the customer. An upright posture and maintaining eye contact convey confidence and competence.

2. Engaging the Customer: Body language can be a powerful tool for engaging the customer. Expressive hand gestures and using gestures to emphasize key points can keep the attention and make the conversation more engaging.

3. Communicating Interest: Your body language can communicate your genuine interest in the customer and their needs. A sincere smile, leaning slightly towards the customer, and active listening can make the customer feel important and heard.

4. Managing Objections: Your body language can assist in handling objections. An open and reassuring posture can alleviate the customer's concerns, while defensive non-verbal communication can worsen the situation.

Methods to Improve Body Language:

1. Maintain an Upright Posture: Stand or sit with your back straight. An upright posture communicates confidence and professionalism. Avoid crossing your arms or adopting closed positions that may appear defensive.

2. Maintain Eye Contact: Eye contact is essential for communicating confidence and interest. Look the customer in the eyes during the conversation, without staring fixedly or intimidatingly.

3. Manage Gestures: Use gestures effectively to emphasize your key points. However, avoid excessive use of gestures that can be distracting or seem nervous.

4. Be Aware of Your Facial Expression: A sincere smile is one of the most effective ways to create a positive connection with the customer. Maintain an open and friendly expression during the conversation.

5. Actively Listen: Show your interest through your facial expression and body language. Lean slightly towards the customer to demonstrate attention.

6. Avoid Distractions: Avoid distracting behaviors such as checking your phone or looking elsewhere while interacting with the customer. This can make the customer feel that you are not engaged in the conversation.

Conclusion:

The seller's body language is an essential component in communication and the art of selling. Your posture, gestures, and facial expression can make a difference in building trust, engaging the customer, and effectively managing objections. With constant practice and increased awareness of your body language, you can significantly improve your non-verbal communication skills and increase your chances of success in sales. Never underestimate the power of your body language in shaping positive perceptions and relationships with customers.

Chapter 10 - Punctuality and Reliability: The Foundation of Credibility and Trust

We explore the two essential qualities for every successful salesperson: punctuality and reliability. These pillars are fundamental to building and maintaining positive relationships with customers, creating trust, and ensuring long-term success.

The Importance of Punctuality:

The customer takes time out of their day to meet you in the store or office. They would be dismayed to find a closed door during your opening hours.

1. Respect for the Customer's Time: Punctuality shows that you respect the customer's time. If you have set an appointment or a meeting, the customer expects you to be present and ready at the agreed time.

2. Creating a Good Impression: Being punctual creates a positive first impression. It demonstrates that you are organized, reliable, and respectful of the customer's expectations.

3. Efficiency in Operation: Being punctual also helps in managing your time. If you follow a precise schedule, you have more time to dedicate to customers and negotiations.

Example of Punctuality:

Imagine having an appointment with a customer at 10:00 AM. You arrive a few minutes early to ensure that you are ready. When the customer arrives exactly at the appointed time, they find you already available and ready to welcome them. This punctuality creates a good impression and opens the door to effective communication from the start.

The Importance of Reliability:

Reliability is another crucial pillar in sales. It's about keeping the promises made to customers and respecting agreed terms. That's why reliability is so important:

1. Building Trust: Reliability is fundamental to building trust. Customers need to know they can count on you to deliver what you promised, at the promised time.

2. Satisfied Customer: When you are reliable, the customer is more likely to be satisfied with your services or products. Your ability to keep promises contributes to ensuring a positive transaction.

3. Respect for the Customer: Showing reliability is a sign of respect for the customer. It means you value their trust and have the integrity to honor your commitments.

Example of Reliability:

Imagine promising a customer that you will deliver their order within a week. If you keep this promise and deliver the product on the agreed day, the customer will feel respected and satisfied. This reliability will contribute to building a trust relationship and could lead to further sales opportunities.

The Winning Combination: Punctuality and Reliability

The combination of punctuality and reliability is what sets successful salespeople apart. These qualities show that you are a customer-oriented professional who respects others' time and honors commitments. Here are some guidelines to maintain and improve your punctuality and reliability:

1. Planning: Organize your day efficiently, taking into account appointments and commitments made with customers.

2. Clear Communication: If you encounter an unforeseen event or delay, communicate it promptly to the customer and propose alternative solutions.

3. Act with Integrity: Be a man of your word. Respect the promises made to customers and keep agreements.

4. Personal Growth: Continue to improve your time management and planning skills to become increasingly reliable.

Conclusion:

Punctuality and reliability are essential for long-term success in the field of sales. These qualities contribute to creating a good impression, building trust, and ensuring that customers are satisfied with their experiences. Always remember that respect for time and integrity in promises are the foundation upon which every successful customer relationship is built.

Chapter 11 - Customize the Product or Service: The Art of Creating Unique Experiences

Let's discover together the importance of customizing products and services in sales. Customization is a winning strategy that meets the specific needs of customers and creates memorable experiences. We will examine examples of how to customize both products and services for maximum impact.

The Importance of Customization:

Customization is the key to creating an authentic connection with customers. Whether you're selling products or services, the ability to adapt what you offer to the individual needs and desires of customers can make the difference between a transaction and a long-term relationship. That's why customization is essential:

1. Meeting Customer Needs: Every customer is unique and has different needs. Customizing the product or service allows you to meet exactly what the customer is looking for.

2. Creating Memorable Experiences: Customization creates unforgettable experiences. When a customer receives a product or service that has been specially designed for them, they feel special and valued.

3. Differentiating from Competition: Customization helps you stand out from the competition. If you can offer something unique and tailored, customers will be more likely to choose you over your competitors.

Examples of Product Customization:

1. Creating a Custom Logo: If you're selling a product that's already in circulation, you can stand out by customizing the product with a unique logo or image. For example, if you sell clothing, you can create a custom logo to print on each garment.

2. Customized Packaging: The product packaging can make a difference. Personalize the box with the customer's name or a special message. This attention to detail makes the customer feel special from the moment they open the box.

3. Customized User Guide: If your product requires instructions, create a customized user guide with the customer's name and tips on how to get the most out of the product.

4. Product Usage Images: If possible, show images of the product being used by satisfied customers. This will help the customer visualize themselves using the product and understand its benefits.

Examples of Service Customization:

1. Offering a Special Welcome: When the customer enters your office or store, make sure to welcome them in a special way. Offer a coffee or a drink, seat the customer comfortably, and make the environment hospitable.

2. Unique Business Cards: Business cards are an effective way to leave a lasting impression. Use business cards in unique materials like plastic or metal. These cards stand out from the others and are more likely to be kept and shown to friends and family by the customer.

Conclusion:

Customization is a key to success in sales. When you customize your products or services, you show the customer that you truly care about meeting their needs and that you are willing to make the extra effort to do so. This attention to detail can create trustful relationships and customer loyalty, leading to a loyal clientele and continued success in the world of sales. It's the details that make the difference.

Chapter 12 - The Importance of Avoiding Inappropriate Jokes in Sales

Together, let's address the topic of inappropriate jokes, particularly those of a sexual nature and those that could personally offend the customer. This chapter highlights how careful management of words and behavior is fundamental for building positive relationships and maintaining a respectful environment in sales.

Why Avoiding Inappropriate Jokes is Crucial:

1. Creating a Respectful Environment: In any professional setting, it's essential to maintain a respectful work environment. Inappropriate jokes can create tensions and inappropriate behavior, making it difficult to establish trustful relationships.

2. Risk of Offending the Customer: Jokes of a sexual nature or that are offensive can easily offend the customer. Providing a positive sales experience means avoiding comments or behaviors that could make the customer feel uncomfortable or disrespected.

3. Preserving Your Reputation: As a seller, your reputation is one of your most valuable assets. Inappropriate jokes can severely damage your image and compromise your credibility.

Examples of Inappropriate Jokes to Avoid:

1. Sexual Jokes: Avoid any comments of a sexual nature, including jokes or innuendos. Even if you think it might be accepted as a joke, it's better not to take risks.

2. Jokes About Customers: Avoid making jokes about other customers, such as comments on their physical appearance, age, or ethnicity. These types of jokes can be extremely offensive, and the customer will think you will do the same behind their back.

3. Political or Religious Jokes: Avoid entering into political or religious discussions with the customer. Political and religious opinions are often personal and can easily lead to controversy.

4. Jokes About the Customer's Personal Situation: Avoid making comments or jokes about the customer's personal situation, such as their marital status, financial situation, or family.

How to Maintain a Professional Tone:

1. Focus on the Customer: Always put the customer at the center of your attention. Listen to their needs, respect their privacy, and ask appropriate questions to better understand their situation.

2. Be Aware of Cultural Differences: Inappropriate jokes can vary from culture to culture. When working with customers from different cultures, try to be sensitive to their sensibilities and customs.

3. Plan Your Communication: Before meeting a customer, plan your communication so that it is professional and respectful. Avoid improvising comments that could turn out to be inappropriate.

4. Maintain an Appropriate Tone of Voice: Your tone of voice and body language can convey your respect and professionalism. Keep a calm and professional tone of voice during interactions with the customer.

Conclusion:

In conclusion, avoiding inappropriate jokes is crucial for maintaining a professional and respectful environment in sales. Jokes of a sexual nature or that are offensive can easily damage your reputation and harm relationships with customers. By maintaining a respectful and attentive approach to communication, you can help build solid and lasting relationships with your clientele.

Chapter 13 - Well-Groomed Appearance, Appropriate Attire, and Accessories: Your Personal Presentation

A well-groomed appearance, appropriate clothing, and accessories in your personal presentation make a big difference in a conversation. Your personal image is a fundamental component of success in sales, as it creates a lasting first impression and communicates professionalism. We will examine examples of how you can take care of your physical appearance and choose suitable clothing and accessories to impress your clients.

The Importance of a Well-Groomed Appearance:

Taking care of one's physical appearance is the starting point for an effective personal presentation. A well-groomed appearance conveys attention to detail and reflects your commitment to professional presentation. Here's why a well-groomed appearance is important:

1. First Impression: The first impression counts a lot in sales. When you present yourself with a well-groomed appearance, you create a positive impression right from the start.

2. Confidence: When you take care of your physical appearance, you convey confidence. This is particularly important because customers are more likely to trust someone who appears confident and competent.

3. Professionalism: Your personal image communicates your level of professionalism. A well-groomed appearance is a sign of respect for the customer and yourself.

Examples of Taking Care of Appearance:

1. Haircut and Beard: Maintain a clean and neat haircut. If you have a beard, make sure it is well-groomed and tidy. Visit a hairdresser or barber regularly.

2. Personal Hygiene: Personal hygiene is essential. Make sure to wash regularly, maintain good dental hygiene, and use fragrances moderately.

The Importance of Appropriate Attire:

Clothing is a crucial aspect of your personal presentation. Appropriate attire communicates your respect for the customer and the professional context you are in. Here's why appropriate attire is important:

1. Represents Your Company: Appropriate attire also represents the company you work for. It is important to respect the company's dress code and convey a cohesive image.

2. Comfort and Adaptation: Appropriate attire should be comfortable and suited to the occasion. Ensure that your clothes make you feel confident and comfortable.

Examples of Appropriate Attire:

1. Professional Attire: If you work in a formal environment, like a financial company, professional attire such as a suit is essential. For less formal sectors, like marketing or technology, business casual attire may be more suitable.

2. Clean and Ironed Outfit: Ensure that your clothes are always clean and ironed. Wrinkled or dirty clothes can convey an image of neglect.

The Importance of Accessories:

Accessories can make a difference in your personal presentation. A well-chosen accessory can add a touch of personality and style to your attire. Here's why accessories are important:

1. Personality and Style: Accessories like a watch, tie, bag, or shoes can reflect your personality and style. Choose accessories that make you feel confident and comfortable.

2. Elegance and Professionalism: Accessories can also enhance your elegance and professionalism. A quality watch, for example, can convey a sense of class and attention to detail.

Conclusion:

In conclusion, a well-groomed appearance, appropriate attire, and accessories are essential elements of your personal presentation in sales. These details communicate professionalism, respect for the customer, and attention to detail. Take care of your personal image and ensure you are always well-prepared when meeting clients.

End

We have reached the end of this journey. I address you, dear reader, with gratitude for dedicating your time and attention to these pages. I hope that you have found valuable information, practical tips, and inspiration in this book to improve your sales skills.

Remember that selling is much more than a commercial transaction; it is about building lasting relationships and creating meaningful experiences for customers. Whether you are an experienced salesperson or just beginning your journey, there is always room for improvement and continuous learning.

I sincerely hope that you can put into practice what you have learned in these pages and achieve the success you deserve in the world of sales. Never forget the importance of trust, professionalism, and empathy in building successful relationships with your customers.

Thank you again for choosing to read this book. I wish you every success in your sales career and sincerely hope to meet you again in the future, in the next books.
Good sales and see you soon!

www.ingramcontent.com/pod-product-compliance
Lightning Source LLC
LaVergne TN
LVHW051206080426
835508LV00021B/2833